ISBN 978-0-282-60168-3
PIBN 10855758

1 MONTH OF
FREE
READING

at
www.ForgottenBooks.com

By purchasing this book you are eligible for one month membership to ForgottenBooks.com, giving you unlimited access to our entire collection of over 1,000,000 titles via our web site and mobile apps.

To claim your free month visit:
www.forgottenbooks.com/free855758

English
Français
Deutsche
Italiano
Español
Português

www.forgottenbooks.com

Mythology Photography **Fiction**
Fishing Christianity **Art** Cooking
Essays Buddhism Freemasonry
Medicine **Biology** Music **Ancient
Egypt** Evolution Carpentry Physics
Dance Geology **Mathematics** Fitness
Shakespeare **Folklore** Yoga Marketing
Confidence Immortality Biographies
Poetry **Psychology** Witchcraft
Electronics Chemistry History **Law**
Accounting **Philosophy** Anthropology
Alchemy Drama Quantum Mechanics
Atheism Sexual Health **Ancient History**
Entrepreneurship Languages Sport
Paleontology Needlework Islam
Metaphysics Investment Archaeology
Parenting Statistics Criminology
Motivational

O

THE LIFE

OF

SAINT GRELLAN,

PATRON OF THE O'KELLYS,

AND OF THE

TRIBES OF HY-MAINE.

BY THE

REV. JOHN O'HANLON, M.R.I.A.

Dublin:

JAMES DUFFY & SONS, 15 WELLINGTON QUAY,

AND 1A PATERNOSTER ROW, LONDON.

1881.

DUBLIN :
PRINTED BY BURKE AND GALLINAGH,
61 & 62 GREAT STRAND STREET.

Dedication.

———◆———

TO THE

RECOGNISED LIVING REPRESENTATIVE

OF HIS

DISTINGUISHED FAMILY AND NAME,

CORNELIUS J. O'KELLY,

Count of the Holy Roman Empire,

CALLAGH CASTLE, COUNTY OF GALWAY,

The Present Memoir

OF HIS PATRON SAINT

IS RESPECTFULLY DEDICATED

BY THE AUTHOR.

LIFE OF ST. GRELLAN.

BESIDES the universal reverence and love, with which Ireland regards the memory of her great Apostle, St. Patrick, most of our provincial districts and their families of distinction have patron saints, for whom a special veneration is entertained. Among the latter, St. Grellan's name is connected with his favoured locality. The extensive territory of Hy-Many is fairly defined,[1] by describing the northern line as running from Bally-moe, county of Galway, to Lanesborough, at the head of Lough Ree, on the River Shannon, and in the county of Roscommon. It extended nearly due east and west, taking in all the southern part of this last-named county. The eastern boundary ran along the River Shannon's course, from Lanesborough to Scariff, in Clare county, and west of Lough Derg. Thence, the southern and western boundaries proceeded by Feaele, on Lough Graney, county of Clare, and passed some distance west of Loughrea to Athenry; thence, they continued through Killererin parish, near Tuam, and on to Ballymoe. All of these last-mentioned localities are situated within the

---

[1] See "The Topographical Poems of John O'Dubhagain and Giolla na Naomh O'Huidhrin," edited by John O'Donovan, LL.D., M.R.I.A. In this work may be found O'Dubhagain's poetical description of this territory, in the original Irish, with the editor's translation, at pp. 68 to 73, with the explanatory notes, 338 to 362, pp. xliv. to xlvi.

county of Galway.[1]　　The earliest noted aboriginal inhabitants of this great extent of country were the Firbolgs, who were also a race of people tributary to the Kings of Connaught.[2] These are thought to have been the successors of Partholan and his followers, who are regarded as being the earliest colonists of Ireland;[3] but all of whom perished in a great plague that came into the island.[4] Before this occurred, however, their rule had been disturbed by the Fomorians, thought to have been pirates from Africa. The northern as well as eastern nations most generally commenced their historic pedigree with a deity; or at least, they ascribe to their first founders heroic qualities or virtues, closely bordering on the possession of supernatural powers. So have we a variety of bardic stories, giving very circumstantial accounts, regarding the migrations of our ancient colonists; but, we have good reasons for supposing those narratives are largely mythological in character. Legends are framed for the acts of our earlier

[1] According to an accurate map of this district, prefixed to the "Tribes and Customs of Hy-Many," by Mr. O'Donovan, the foregoing lines and places designated the former boundaries of that territory. The Irish tract in question was edited by him, from a copy in the Book of Lecan, fol. 90 to 92. An English translation, with notes, he has also given.

[2] It was supposed, by John O'Donovan, that the Book of Hy-Many was in the possession of a private collector in England, A.D. 1843, and that it was a distinct compilation from what had been published.

[3] According to the O'Clerys, following the chronology of the Septuagint, Partholan arrived, A.M. 2520 years. Sir Dr. O'Donovan's "Annals of the Four Masters," vol. i. pp. 4, 5.

[4] Dr. Jeoffrey Keating, who quotes the Psalter of Cashel and Ninus, gives an account of this expedition. See Dermod O'Connors, Keating's "General History of Hreland," part i.

heroes, as history fails to shed light on their period, now so remote from our own times.

About the year of the world 2029,[1] a Scythian[2] hero, known as Nemed or Nenidh, signifying "the holy one," brought a number of colonists with him into Ireland. He is said to have been remotely related to Partholan, if not a direct descendant. His name has been Latinized in latter days into Nemethus or Nemidius. With four sons, and a fleet of thirty-four ships, each containing thirty persons, he arrived in Ireland, from the Euxine Sea. Finding the island without inhabitants, these took possession and settled therein; at the same time, they began to clear away the thick woods in many places, and to improve the soil by cultivation.[3] We are told, likewise, that Nemed employed master-builders, distinguished by the name Fomhoraicc, to erect royal seats for his purpose. After a time, his people were much annoyed by pirates called Fomorians. These wasted the coasts by their inroads, and the interior they even harassed. Nemed fought four battles with them; he was successful in the first three; but he was defeated in the last battle, when his son Art, who had been born in Ireland, was slain, with most of his people.[4] This so afflicted the king that he died of grief.[5] Should we follow the authority of bardic history, the Nemedians were exterminated. Ireland was again left

[1] See O'Flaherty's "Ogygia," Pars. ii. p. 65.
[2] See Sir James Ware's "De Hibernia et Antiquitatibus ejus Disquisitiones," Cap. ii., p. 6.
[3] According to Dr. Jeoffrey Keating.
[4] See L'Abbé Ma-Geoghegan's "Histoire de l'Irlande." Tome i., chap. iii. p. 60.
[5] See Sir William Betham's "The Gael and Cymbri," p. 427.

to its native woods, and a wilderness[1] during two hundred years or more; while, according to certain computations, four hundred and twelve years[2] passed away, before it was again inhabited. O'Flaherty does not say a word respecting the fate of the Foghmoraicc,[3] by some confounded with the Fomorians, and by others distinguished from them. After a succession of ages, the Scuits, Scythians, or Scots, who had migrated to Ireland, are also called Gaidelians and Phenians; while these appellations denote a mixture of Celts, Scythians, and Pœnicians from that part of the Continent whence these arrived.[4] In the remote periods, dialectic incorporations were common among the Celts and Scythians, especially in Spain, where the latter settled, and whence the Scoto-Milesian colony came.

Frequent mention of the Firbolgs, or Bolgæ, occurs in our ancient Irish poems and annals. Whether they preceded or followed the Celts in Ireland has been a matter of controversy among modern historians.[5]

The Firbolgs are called also Sial m Bolgæ, and Slioght m Bealidh. These people were invaded by the Tuatha De Dananu, known as the People of the Gods of Dananu, daughter of Dalbaoit, and said to have been descended from Nemed. Her sons are thought to have

---

[1] See William F. Skene's "Celtic Scotland : a History of Ancient Alban," Vol. i., Book i., chap. iv. p. 173.

[2] See O'Flaherty's "Ogygia," Pars ii. p. 73.

[3] See Wood's "Inquiry concerning the Primitive Inhabitants of Ireland." Introduction, p. 17.

[4] See Mr. Charles O'Conor's "Dissertations on the Origin and Antiquities of the Ancient Scots," p. xxx.

[5] See Thomas Moore's "History of Ireland," Vol. i. chap. i. pp. 2, 3.

been famous for sorceries and necromantic powers, which arts were communicated to their descendants. The Tuatha De Danann are thought to have invaded Ireland A.M. 2737.[1] Regarding the origin of the name Bolgæ, however, the learned are far from agreeing in their opinions; but various statements have been ventured upon by different writers, from the early to our own days. A received opinion is, that they came from Britain; but, from what particular part of it has not been determined. A Belgic origin has been assigned to them, likewise, and it has been supposed originally they were of German or Gothic extraction.[2] If such were the case, their previous manners and customs are best revealed in the descriptions left us by the early classic writers, aided by modern investigators.[3] Some think that by Clan Bolus are meant the Belgæ of Britain, who, having passed over from Belgium, or from Lower Germany, spread themselves over the countries of Somerset, Wilton, and the interior of Haverford; and that the British language, which they made use of in Ireland was eloquently and expressively designated Belgaid, intimating it to be a Belgic idiom. Another supposition has it, that the name Firbolg is connected with superstition, and derived from the worship which this people paid their gods. For, in the language of the

---

[1] According to Keating and O'Flaherty. The Four Masters' computation have it at A.M. 3303.

[2] Sir William Wilde's "Beauties of the Boyne and its Tributary Blackwater," chap. ix. p. 218.

[3] In this connexion the late Emperor of the French, Napoleon III., has left us a very interesting account of the Belgæ and of the Gaulish Celts, in his "Histoire de Jules César," Tome ii. Lio. iii. chap. ii. pp. 13-44.

Celts, the Germans, and all the northern nations, it is
thought, that Bel stood for Sol or Apollo, the sun ; and
this deity was indiscriminately called Bal, Beal, and
Sol, intimating his dominion as lord of the world. This
idea they are said to have received from the Phœnicians,
the authors of such superstition, who in the excess of
their false zeal, scrupled not to offer human sacrifices to
their Baal, though he afterwards condescended to
acquiesce in the substitution of brute immolation.[1]
Others would have them called Bolgæ, from *bolg*, " a
quiver," as excelling in archery; others state *bolg*
means a "leathern pouch," or "bag;" others deduce
their name from the Irish word *bol*, "a poet," or "sage,"
as they were eminent in these respective characters.
Another ingenious derivation of the name,[2] found in
the Irish version of Nennius,[3] *Viri Bullorum*, sug-
gests a possibility of their having been so designated,
because they carried shepherd's crooks.[4]

If we follow the accounts of certain writers, those
people were distinguished into three nations, or tribes
viz., Firbolgæ,[5] Firdomnan,[6] and Firgalion,[7] generally

[1] See that insipid, ill-digested, and ridiculously pedantic compilation called "Phenician Ireland," edited by Henry O'Brien, Esq.,
A.B., and which professes to be the translation of some Latin papers
on Irish History, by a learned Spaniard, Doctor Joachimus Laurentius
Villaneuva, chap. xxii. pp. 209-212. Hence the first of May is called
in Irish, La Beal—that is, the "day of the fire Beal."

[2] By Rev. Dr. James Henthorn Todd.

[3] The "Historia Britonum," so well known. This version was
edited by Dr. Todd and the Hon. Algernon Herbert.

[4] See p. 44, note (r.) Du Cange asserts that *Bullum*, in the Latinity
of the middle ages, signified " baculum pastoris."

[5] Also called by Nennius *Viri Bullorum*.

[6] Also called by Nennius *Viri Dominiorum*.

[7] Also called by Nennius *Viri Armorum*.

interpreted, Clan Bulus, Clan Domnan, and Clan Gallon. These are said to have been of Nemed's race.

The Firbolg, or Bolgæ, are thought to have established themselves at first in the neighbourhood of Wexford and Wicklow, on the south-east of Ireland. These Teutonic people are said to have divided the whole island into five great provinces, over which they established a sort of royal sway.[1]

A colony of Firbolgs, it would appear, had been settled in the district of Hy-Many, province of Connaught, even before the introduction of the Christian religion, and probably for a long time previous to the beginning of the fifth century. The Firbolgs, as also the Tuatha De Danann tribes of Ireland, were accustomed to build not only their fortresses and sepulchres, but also their houses of stone, without cement, and in the style, now usually called Cyclopean and Pelasgic.[2] The Firbolgs were certainly in Hy-Many during the reign of Duach Gallach, who was supreme ruler over these parts.

It has been said, that the literal meaning of Iath Maine is the country or inheritance of Maneus, who first gave it a distinctive appellation; and, as we are told, this territory takes its origin from Maney-Mor, or Maneus the Great, one of the Milesian race, who conquered—about the year of Christ, 450—the former inhabitants of that very considerable portion of Connaught—an extent of country which from him afterwards retained the name of Imaney. This celebrated chieftain was

[1] See Elias Regnault's " Histoire de l'Irlande," chap. ii. p. 20.
[2] See Dr. George Petrie's " Ecclesiastical Architecture and Round Towers of Ireland," Part ii. sect. ii. p. 127.

the first of his race, who embraced the Christian faith in the western parts of Ireland.

Kellach, King of Imaney, was a prince, renowned for his valour and deeds of arms. One of his lineal descendants was Maney-Mor, who flourished towards the year 920. From his proper name was formed the patronymic name of O'Kelly,[1] which signifies grandson or descendant, of Kellach ;[2] for, as we are informed, about the eleventh century, Irish chiefs began to adopt family names in order to distinguish more exactly their posterity, and the particular scions of each family.

The chiefs of the tribe of Imaney were successively styled kings, princes, or chieftains, or simply O'Kelly or O'Maney-Mor. These two names, held as titles, denoted the chief of the clan or tribe of the O'Kellys. They served as war-cries in the field, when called to active service.

[1] The most complete account of this family we possess is that contained in the "Tribes and Customs of Hy-Many."

[2] The writer has been favoured by Thomas A. Kelly, Esq., St. Grellan's, Monkstown, County Dublin, with the perusal of a very interesting family Manuscript. It is intituled, "Gone Days of I Maney, Memorials of Clan-Kellae, (an Tuir an Dia,) or of the Sept, Clan, or Tribe of the O'Kellys of the Tower of God, whose chiefs were successively styled Kings, Princes, and Chieftains, or Lords of Imaney or South Connact, in Ireland—present county of Galway—Hereditary Marshals of the Province of Connact. Drawn up from the National Records of Ireland and family papers of the Branch af Skryne, or Athlone Branch, Chief of the Name. By Charles Denis Count O'Kelly Farrell, 1850." This work is learnedly and laboriously compiled, while it contains coloured drawings of the O'Kellys' armorial devices, with a very complete history of the family, and from the earliest times. We hope it may be published, as a valuable record of men and deeds almost as yet buried in oblivion, but deserving a niche among our national archives.

Independent in all their rights of jurisdiction,[1] they however acknowledged the priority of the provincial King of Connaught, in conformity with the federative system of Ireland. When the province was engaged in a general war, the chief, O'Kelly, exercised the heredi-   /. tary office of Marshal, or General of the Connaught armies.

In the national wars against the Danes and Northmen, as afterwards against the English, the O'Kellys signalized themselves by their patriotism and intrepidity. For their patron saint, they manifested a singular devotion.

It is to be regretted, that so few biographical particulars have been given, in the only brief accounts we can find, regarding the Patron of Hy-Many. A very ancient copy of St. Grellan's Life is quoted by Duald Mac Firbis, in his Genealogical Book, as a proof of the existence of the Firbolgs in the province of Connaught, after the period of the introduction of Christianity; and, also, it is cited, by Gratianus Lucius, in his "Cambrensis Eversus," as a proof of the fact, which he thinks it establishes, namely, that the ancient Irish paid tithes.[2] No vellum copy of this Life is now in Dublin. There is an Irish Life of St. Grellan in paper, and transcribed by Brother Michael O'Clery. It is kept in a thick quarto volume, among the Manuscripts

---

[1] Of Hy-Maine we find O'Kelly styled "supreme lord" in Roderick O'Flaherty's "Chorographical Description of West or H-Iar Connaught," written in 1684, and edited by James Hardiman, M.R.I.A. Additional Notes, A. p. 146.

[2] See John O'Donovan's Translation of "Tribes and Customs of Hy-Many," p. 8, note (v.)

of the Burgundian Library, at Bruxelles.[1] Besides this
there is a paper copy of his Life[2]—probably containing
similar matter—and preserved in the Royal Irish
Academy, among its manuscripts. This Life of St
Grellan is in a quarto Miscellany of 352 written pages
copied by James Maguire, a good and faithful scribe,[3]
according to Eugene O'Curry. This transcript was
finished, in the year 1721, and in some place called Dubh-
bhaile (Black Town). The pages are written in double
columns, and chiefly Lives of Saints are to be found in it.
The Life of St. Greallan is contained there, from page
235 to 240.[4]

The usual name given to this holy man is Grellan, or
Greallain, in Irish, and this has been Latinized into
Grellanus. Dr. Lynch writes of him as Orillan,[5] when
alluding to this Patron of Hy-Many, in his celebrated
work.

According to the accounts we have of the saint, he
was a contemporary with St. Patrick, and he must have
flourished about the close of the fifth century. He is
classed among the Irish Apostle's disciples,[6] and this
too is stated, in the tenth chapter of his own Life.[7] He

[1] Classed Vol. XI., fol. 83. This Manuscript appears to have been
written in the years 1628 and 1629. It contains 270 folios.

[2] The quarto paper MS., classed No. 33.5.

[3] This appears from an entry at p. 100.

[4] The transcript of this Life was finished, on the 10th day of
January, 1720, as an appended Irish notice declares.

[5] See "Cambrensis Eversus," edited by Rev. Dr. Kelly. Vol. ii.
chap. xv. pp. 260 to 263.

[6] Letter of Very Rev. Canon Ulick J. Bourke, P.P., Claremorris,
Co. Mayo, dated 7th March, 1879.

[7] See "Martyrology of Donegal," edited by Rev. Drs. Todd and
Reeves, at the 10th of November, pp. 302, 303.

also obtained the episcopal rank, being renowned for his sanctity and miracles.

His father's name was Cuillin, son of Cairbre Cluais-derg,[1] of the Lagenians, while Eithne was the name of his mother. He was born in the time of St. Patrick, as the first chapter of his Irish Life states,[2] and a legend is there introduced, as serving to illustrate the prognostications of his subsequent distinguished career, and specially accompanying the event of his birth.

In the time of Lugaidh [3] Mac Laoighaire Mac Neill, a great thunder-storm was heard by all the men of Erinn, and they were astonished at its unusual loudness. They asked Patrick, the son of Alpin, what it portended. He answered, that Greallan was then born, and that he had been only six months in his mother's womb, at the time. Hence, we may infer, that he came into the world about the middle or towards the close of the fifth century. Wars and commotions are said to have prevailed in Ireland, at the advent of our saint's birth. We are told, likewise, that Greallan had been fostered by one named Cairbre, probably a relation among his family connexions.

Among the many other cares of his Mission, St. Patrick took charge of Greallan's education, and made him a companion. He enrolled this young disciple amongst his brethren, taking him to Ath-Cliath, Dublinne,[4]

[1] Or as Anglicised, Cairbre of the Red Ears.

[2] See "Martyrology of Donegal," edited by Rev. Drs. Todd and Reeves, pp. 302, 303, at the 10th of November.

[3] His reign over Ireland was from A.D. 479 to 503, or twenty-five years, according to the chronology of the Four Masters.

[4] In English it means, "the ford of the hurdles of the black pool." This is said to have been the ancient name for the present Metropolis of Ireland, and since known as Dublin.

when he went there. This must have been after the
middle of the fifth century. Then is quoted a poem, in
which St. Patrick said, that a noble person should be in
the land of Leinster. This promise was an allusion to
our saint, whose purity and virtues are there praised.

A kinsman to the celebrated Colla da Chrioch chieftains in Ulster possessed great influence in Hy-Many,
a territory of the Firbolgs, in the time of St. Patrick,
when he is said to have visited Echin, the son of
Briain,[1] son to Eachach, King of Connaught. Eachin
refused to be converted,[2] but all his brothers embraced
the faith. Eoghan, who was son to Duach Gallach,[3]
one of Eachin's brothers, was afterwards baptised by St.
Grellan. On this occasion a great miracle was wrought,
at a place called Achadh Fionnabhrach. When only a
child, Eoghan had died, to the inexpressible grief of his
parents. However, when St. Grellan beheld this
afflicting state of affairs, he raised his staff, and then
applied it to the body of their child. This touch caused
him to be resuscitated, and it impressed a mark on their
son, which was afterwards visible. As a consequence, he
bore the name, by which he was best known, namely,
Eoghan Scriabh, or "Owen the Striped."[4] The mira-

[1] He is said to have had four-and-twenty sons. Among these, we
find the names of Echin, or Echenna, Duach Gallach, Fergussius,
Eochad, Ercus Derg, Æongussius, Ball-Derg, Tenedus, and Muchitius.

[2] His wife and children also refused baptism ; yet, afterwards, she
sought to be reconciled with the Irish Apostle, and her husband,
Echen, was baptised by St. Benignus. See this whole account, taken
from a Life of the latter, in Colgan's "Trias Thaumaturga," Appendix
iii. ad Acta S. Patricii, pp. 203, 204.

[3] He is called "frater junior de filiis Briain."

[4] "St. Greallan's Irish Life," chap. iii. See "Martyrology of
Donegal," edited by Rev. Drs. Todd and Reeves, pp. 302, 303.

culous crozier was thenceforward held in great veneration.
It is said, that Duach Gallach was a Christian, having
been baptised by St. Patrick, while the wife of Echin,
called Fortrui, was aunt to St. Benignus,[1] a favourite
disciple of the Irish Apostle. The latter proclaimed
that he should be a king, and that from his race kings
should proceed. In fine, Eachin was baptised at Kilbennin,
near Tuam.[2]

At Achadh Fionnabhrach, Duach Gallach bestowed a
tract of land, and he gave possession of it to St. Grellan.
The name was even changed—owing to this peen-
liarity of circumstance—from Achadh Fionnabhrach
to that of Craobh Greallain, which signifies, the "Branch
of Grellan." This name is said in his Irish Life to have
been owing to a branch, which Duach and St. Patrick
gave our saint in token of possession. Here, east of
Magh-Luirg, this saint is said to have built a Church,
before the arrival of Maine-Mor in Connaught. When
alluding to Craobh Ghreallain, Mr. O'Curry remarks,
that he believed its precise situation was not known.[3]

As a token of the veneration for our saint, Duach
required that every chieftain's wife should give seven
garments, as a tribute to Grellan; and, for payment of
this ecclesiastical assessment, the guarantee of St.
Patrick had been asked and obtained afterwards by
the local Patron.

[1] He was the son of Sesonean, a disciple of St. Patrick; and his
mother was called Sadelina, descended from Cather, King of Leinster.

[2] See Very Rev. Ulick J. Bourke's "Aryan Origin of the Gaelic
Race and Language," chap. xiii. pp. 408, 409.

[3] See a brief description of this specified Life of St. Greallain in the
"Catalogue of Irish Manuscripts of the Royal Irish Academy," by
Eugene O'Curry. First Series, Vol. ii. pp. 445, 446.

A romantic and, as there are good reasons for supposing, a very questionable narrative of particulars
regarding the conquest of Hy-Many by Maine-Mor and
the Colla da Chrioch's race is given, in the Life of our
Saint. We are there told, that Eochaidh Ferdaghiall,
father to Maine-Mor, took counsel with his son as to
how the Colla da Chrioch tribe, over whom they ruled,
should be able to procure a sufficient scope of territory
for their numerous and increasing population.

Then they held possession of Oirghialla, with the
hostages of this place, and of Ulidia. It was generally
allowed, that quarrels might break out amongst the chiefs
of this ascendant tribe, were they to be confined within
any one province. But, considering the Firbolgic territory of Hy-Many as a fair object for a predatory excur-
sion, and as it had been thinly inhabited, they resolved
on securing a considerable portion of it by conquest.

Under the leadership of Maine-Mor, the enterprising
Colla da Crioch assembled their forces at Clogher, in
the county of Tyrone, and then they proceeded in battle
array, towards the territory of Hy-Many. This nomadic
tribe—for such it had now become—collected the
herds and flocks, which belonged to them; and these
animals were driven on their line of march by the
invading host, who set out in quest of new settlements.
Crossing the Shannon, they came to Druim Clasach, and
plundered all that district of country, lying between
Lough Ree and the River Suck. They also despatched
messengers to Cian, Chief of the Firbolgs, who dwelt
at a place called Magh-Seincheineoil. The English
equivalent to this is, " the plain of the old tribe," probably in allusion to the aboriginal colony there settled.

The length and breadth of the plain was from Dun-
na-riogh to the river of ·Bairrduin, and from Ath-
n-fasdoig to Ath-dearg-duin, which was afterwards
called Ath-an-Chorrdhaire.[1] They required from him
tribute and territory. This unjust demand he refused,
and he also prepared to resist. He raised a force of
3,000,[2] or, as some accounts have it, of 4,000 Firbolgs,[3]
armed with swords, bucklers, and helmets.[4] These
dwelt in the plain of Magh Seincheineoil.[5] At their
head, Cian marched to meet the invaders.

About this time, St. Grellan, who had journeyed over
the territory of Hy-Many, came to a place, denominated
Cill Cluaine, and now called Kilclooney, in the neighbourhood of Ballinasloe, and the present barony of
Clonmacowen, County of Galway.

Thus, in a manner, he was placed between the con-
tending forces; and his name and influence seem to
have been respected, by chieftains on both sides. He
was waited upon by Cian, who, in all probability, gave
the saint an exaggerated account, regarding his means
for defence against the invaders. However this may be,
Orellan induced the Colla da Cricch race to enter into
articles of truce with the Firbolgs, and to deliver

[1] The limits of this plain are given, in that portion of the Life of St.
Grellan, quoted by Dr. O'Donovan, in "Tribes and Customs of Hy-
Many," p. 11.

[2] According to Dr. Lynch.

[3] This latter seems to have been the number, according to an old
Irish poem, in the Life of St. Greallan.

[4] See Rev. Dr. Kelly's edition of "Cambrensis Eversus," Vol. ii.
chap. xv. pp. 260, 261.

[5] See an account of the Firbolg possession of Hy-Many, in Eugene
O'Curry's work "On the Manners and Customs of the Ancient Irish,"
edited by Dr. W. K. Sullivan, Vol. iii. sect. xxii. pp. 83, 84.

twenty-seven chiefs of the invading host, as hostages
for the observance of peace. Amhalgaidh, son to Maine,
was one of these hostages, and he was delivered for
keeping to Cian's Brehon. But the Brehon's wife con-
ceived an unlawful passion for this young prince. The
particulars of this affair becoming known to the lawgiver,
he was filled with jealousy and resentment. Having
great influence over the mind of Cian, this latter was
persuaded to murder all his hostages.

It is indeed a difficult matter to understand that
mixture of generosity and ferociousness, which has been
known to characterize the manners of our forefathers.
The wild excesses of barbarity owe their origin to
ungovernable fits of passion, which overcharge man's
nature with the ripe growth of licentiousness. Innate
generosity is overshadowed or extinguished, where
custom sanctions actions of treachery and bloodshed.
The barbarous deed it was designed to put into exe-
cution, during the cover of night and darkness.

However, the most awful punishments are inflicted
by Divine Providence, on the crimes of perfidy and
cruelty, as happened in this case. To complete his
perfidious proceeding, Cian invited the Colla da Crioch
chiefs to a feast, which was prepared, as he said, for them.
His real intention was to surprise them, and at a
moment when they should be least on their guard
against his treacherous designs. With such a purpose
formed, he placed some soldiers in ambuscade, to slay
the expected guests. Religious feeling and principle
are necessary to control heartless savagery. True civilization can only follow, in the wake of Christian morals
and influences, while here too, the miraculous power

possessed by the holy Grellan, and also his prophetic spirit, were rendered manifest to all concerned.

The Colla da Crioch host was then encamped, at the foot of Seisidh-beag, in the territory of Maenmagh. At this time, Eochaidh and Maine were at the foot of Bearnach na n-arm. Having some intimation respecting the design of Cian and of his armed bands, and being apprehensive regarding the violation of a truce to which he was the principal guarantee, St. Grellan perceived ⸲ the armed bands from the door of his church. Raising his hands towards heaven, and beseeching the God of hosts to avert the consequences of such foul treachery from those chiefs who were doomed to destruction, his prayer was heard, as the account declares. The hosts of Cian, with their leader, were swallowed up, and buried beneath the plain, on which they stood. It was suddenly changed into a quagmire, and here they all miserably perished. This place afterwards received the name Magh Liach, *i.e.*, "the plain of sorrow," since it proved such to the perfidious Firbolgs;[1] and, Dr. Lynch declares, that in his day, this marsh was quite impassible either for man or beast.[2] It is said, St. Grellan then informed Maine and his people about this treacherous plot contrived against

[1] "Hodieque invia est; incedentium gressibus ita coedens, ut in ea nec homines nec pecudes vestigia figere possint."—"Cambrensis Eversus," Vol. ii. chap. xv. pp. 260, 262.

[2] Regarding this event, Mr. O'Donovan remarks, "It is to be lamented that no Firbolgic writer survived to relate the true account of this transaction, for every acute investigator of history will be apt to suspect that the treachery was on the side of the conquerors, the Clann Colla. But who would have the courage to write this in the fourteenth century?"—"Tribes and Customs of Hy-Many," p. 12, note (z.)

them, and its signal failure followed in the manner
described. He then counselled them, to take possession
of the Firbolg's territory, to cultivate brotherly love, to
abominate treachery, and to establish a legal rate for
ecclesiastical purposes, by accepting a law imposed on
them by himself. The Clann Colla agreed to his pro-
posals, and Maine desired the saint to name his own
award. In compliance with such request, he is said to
have repeated in the Irish language some verses given
in his Life. These, however, bear intrinsic evidences of
having been extracted from bardic remains, or of
having been composed by his biographer. The following
is the literal English translation, as furnished, from
the original Irish verses, by Dr. John O'Donovan :—

" Great is my tribute on the race of Maine, a screaball (scruple)[1]
      out of every townland.

   Their successes shall be bright and easy ; it is not a tribute
      acquired without cause.
   The first-born of every family to me, that are all baptized
      by me.
   Their tribute paid to me is a severe tribute, every firstling
      pig and firstling lamb.
   To me belongs—may their cattle thence be the more nume-
      rous ;—from the race of Maine, the firstling foal.
   Let them convey their tribute to my church, besides territory
      and land.
   From Dal Druithne I am not entitled to tribute or other
      demands.

[1] In another part of the ''Tribes and Customs of Hy-Many,'' p. 81,
we are told, that "The race of Maine, both women and men, pay a
sgreaball caethrach to St. Grellan." And Mr. O'Donovan, in a note on
the passage, remarks, " Sgreaball caetrach (Sgreaball), which literally
means a scuptulum or scruple, and was at three-pence, is sometimes
indefinitely used to denote any tribute." Here sgreaball caethrach
signifies ''tribute,'' or ''tribute in sheep.''

Their fame is much heard of ; the Muinntir Maeilfinnain belong not to me.

Of all the Hy-Many, these excepted, the tributes and rents are mine.

Let them protect my church for its God. Their chief and his subjects are mine.

Their success and injunctions it was I that ordained, without defect.

While they remain obedient to my will, they shall be victorious in every battle.

Let the warlike chiefs observe the advice of my successor.

And among the Gaels, north and south, their's shall be the unerring director.

Frequent my sacred church, which has protected each refugee.

Refuse not to pay your tribute to me, and you shall receive as I have promised.

My blessing on the agile race, the sons of Maine of chess boards.

That race shall not be subdued, so as they carry my crozier.

Let the battle standard of the race be my crozier of true value.[1]

And battles will not overwhelm them, their successors shall be very great.

" Great," &c.[2]

Afterwards, St. Grellan selected at Kilcloony the site for a church. There he built on a rising ground, or Eiscir, a little distance to the north-west of the Ballinasloe town. Some ruins are yet remaining there, but it should be hazardous to assert the walls date back to the fifth century.

---

[1] In the "Tribes and Customs of Hy-Many," p. 81, it is said of Maine's race, "St. Grellan presides over their battles," i.e., "the crozier of St. Grellan," or some such object is borne in the standard of the King of Hy-Many.

[2] See Mr. O'Donovan's translation, in "Tribes and Customs of Hy-Many," pp. 13, 14.

The Irish were accustomed to impose voluntary assessments of the nature, already indicated by the record we have quoted, to mark their consideration and respect for those distinguished by their ministerial works. It is stated, in the Irish Life of St. Grellan, that he received the first offspring of any brood animal; such as hog, and lamb, and foal, in Hy-Many.[1] These tributes were regularly paid to the successors of the holy man, in the church honoured by his presence and labours during life.

St. Grellan was honoured with particular devotion in the Church of Killcluian, diocese of Clonfert, on the 17th of September.[2] On this day his feast occurs,[3] according to our traditions or Calendars,[4] while he seems to have had a second festival, at the 10th of November.[5] It seems strange, that at neither day he is mentioned in the Feilire of St. Ængus the Culdee, nor is the date for his death recorded in our Annals. However, we may fairly assume, that he lived on, until near the middle of the sixth century.

St. Orellan is the principal patron of those portions

---

[1] The same is stated by Dr. John Lynch, in his "Cambrensis Eversus," p. 186. "E singulis Manachiæ domibus patroni sui S. Grillani success-oribus tres denarii quotannis, primus porculus, primus agnus, et primus equinus, deferrebantur."

[2] Dr. Lynch's "Cambrensis Eversus," Vol. ii. chap. xv. p. 262.

[3] In the "Martyrology of Donegal," edited by Drs. Todd and Reeves, there we find only the simple entry "Greallan, Bishop." See pp. 250, 251.

[4] Whether the entry, "Giallani Epa. o Laind," at this date, in the "Martyrology of Tallaght," edited by Dr. Kelly, have reference to our saint or not, I am unable to determine, yet no other seems there to account for his feast.

[5] See some further notices, at this date, in the "Martyrology of Donegal," pp. 302, 303.

of Galway and Roscommon counties, formerly known by
the designation of Hy-Many; and, for many centuries,
even to the present age, the crozier of St. Grellan had
been preserved in the territory.

Dr. Lynch declares, also, that in his time this pastoral
staff of St. Grellan was held in great veneration.[1]   A
relic of this kind, when used as a standard, was usually
called cathach, *i.e.*, " prœliator,"[2] such as the celebrated
cathach of St. Columkille.[3]

This crozier of St. Grellan was preserved for ages, in
the family of O'Cronghaile, or Cronelly, who were the
ancient Comharbas of the saint. This term of Com-
harba had an ecclesiastical meaning, and generally it
signified successor in a see, church, or monastery; but,
in due course, it had a wider signification, and the
Comhorba was regarded as the vicar—a legal represeu-
tative of the Patron Saint, or founder of the Church.
But, the word *Comhorba* is not exclusively ecclesiastical;
for in the ancient laws of Erin, it meant the heir and
conservator of the inheritance; and, in the latter sense,
it is always used, in our ecclesiastical writings.[4]

[1] See " Cambrensis Eversus," Vol. ii. chap. xv. p. 262.
[2] See Colgan, " Trias Thaumaturga," p. 409. col. 2.   " Et cathach,
id est prœliator, vulge appellatur, fertque traditio quod si circa illius
exercitum, antequam hostem adoriantur tertio cum debita reverentia
circumducatur, eveniat ut victoriam reportet."
[3] Described by Sir Wm. Betham in his "Antiquarian Researches."
[4] In addition to the foregoing, the late Professor Eugene O'Curry,
whose acquaintance with the laws, manners and customs of our an-
cestors, renders his opinions of great weight on a subject of this
nature, has given the following information to the author, and for a
much fuller account, the reader is referred to his " Life of St. Malacy
O'Morgair."—chap. xiii.:—

" There was an understood original compact, recognised by the
' Brehon Laws,' which vested the *Comhorbship* of the Church and its

The shrine of St. Grellan was in existence so late
as the year 1836, it being then in the possession of
a poor man, named John Cronelly, the senior representative of the Comharbas of the saint, who lived near
Abasera, in the east of the county of Galway; but, it is
not to be found now, in that county.[1] It was probably
sold to some collector of antiquities, and it is not now
known to be in the possession of any person; yet, it

lands in two families; namely, in that of the Patron Saint or
founder, and in that of the person who gave the original site and
endowment.

"It was the family of the Patron Saint, that invariably supplied
the Abbot, as long as there could be found among them even a psalm-
singer, to take the office; and, when they failed to supply a fit
person, then he was sought from the family of the owner of the land.
If, in the meantime, a better and more learned man of the Patron's
family should spring up, the abbacy was to be handed over to him;
but, if he were not better, he should wait until it became vacant by
death or otherwise.

"If, however, in the absence of a qualified person from either
family, an unqualified person should succeed as temporal heir, he was
obliged to provide a suitable clergyman to discharge the offices of the
church, according to its dignity, whilst the natural abbot administered
the temporal offices and the management of the land.

"The *Airchinnech* or *Erenach* was a mere temporal agent or
steward of the church lands, under the *Comhorba*, whoever he might
be. He sometimes took the tonsure and some other minor order,
which raised his Eric, or composition, in case of any insult or injury
offered to him. He was generally a married man, without any official
value or reverence of person, but what was derived from the character,
or ecclesiastical dignity of the Patron Saint, whose secular inheritance
he managed. It happened often, however, that the whole adminis-
tration of the Church and its land was performed by one and the
same person. This was when the abbot, bishop, or priest performed
himself the clerical duties, and also acted as his own *Airchinnech* or
steward."

[1] Such is the statement of Canon Ulick J. Bourke, P.P., of Clare
morris, Co. Mayo, in a letter, dated thence March 7th, 1879.

seems incredible, that such an interesting relic could
have been lost, as we have been enabled to ascertain
the fact of its preservation to a comparatively recent
period.

The house of Imaney was known, since the eleventh
century, by the name of O'Kelly. Formerly this
renowned family enjoyed all the rights of sovereignty
in the western parts of Ireland, where they possessed so
very extensive a territory. Even from the invasion of
the English down to the reigns of Mary and Elizabeth,
the chiefs of this house maintained their independence.[1]

At the beginning of the fifteenth century, the house
of O'Kelly divided into four principal branches, each
family of which had for its appanage one of the four
baronies of Kilyan, Athlone, Tiaquin, and Kilconnel;
the southern half-barony of Ballymo falling to the share
of the branch of Kilyan.

The government of Imaney was alternatively exercised
by the chiefs of the first and two last of those branches.
However, that of Kilconnel or Aughrim, though a
younger branch, held in latter times the dignity of
chieftain of the O'Kellys. The principal seat of their
residence was at Aughrim, while their burial place was
at Clonmacnoise, and in latter years they were interred
at Kilconnel.

The chieftains of the Kilconnel or Aughrim O'Kellys
was but titular, at the accession of James I. This
branch was dispersed under Cromwell, and at this day
it is extinct. The branches of Kilyan and Tiaquin, or
Gallagh, also lost the greater part of their properties,

[1] According to Charles Denis Count O'Kelly Farrell's Ms
" Gone Days of I Mainey, Memorials of Clan-Kellae," r '

during the Revolutions of 1641 and of 1688. The present representative of this branch is Count Cornelius J. O'Kelly, of the Holy Roman Empire, now living at Gallagh Castle, near Tuam, and he still retains the ancient Irish title of the O'Maine Mor, or, Chief of Hy-Maine.[1] The chieftains of Athlone or Skryne, whose territory lay still nearer to the English settlements, required all their watchfulness to guard against the common enemy. Those O'Kellys did not lay claim to their rights of alternative government. Wearied at last with disastrous wars, which had retarded the march of civilization in their unfortunate country, they submitted to Mary Queen of England, thus sacrificing their feelings to take a step, which they believed should secure to their posterity civil and religious liberty. However, they found themselves compromised and deceived, under the following reigns.

The Athlone branch of the O'Kellys still possesses part of the ancient principality of Imaney, of which Colonel O'Kelly, its lord, was deprived under Cromwell. He was afterwards reinstated in it by letters patent from Charles II., in reward for services rendered by him to the Royal cause, during the Revolution.

Like most of their countrymen, the O'Kellys were remarkable in every age for their attachment to the faith of their fathers; but abroad were most of their expatriated gentlemen distinguished, in the camps, cabinets, and courts of the Continent. More ample details than the author could be expected to insert, in the present brief Memoir, will be found in that work, to which allusion has been already made—"The Tribes and

[1] See Thom's Directory for 1880, p. 757.

Customs of Hy-Many." There, not only are the O'Kelly's territory, family, and kindred tribes recorded, but, in his Appendices to that Tract, its learned editor has very fully treated regarding personal history and genealogy, which must have an interest for Irishmen, who are anxious to be informed about the career and fortunes of their gallant, adventurous, and enterprising countrymen, at home and abroad.

After a scarcely interrupted struggle during many ages at home, yielding at last to the advantages possessed by an enemy, favoured by more fortunate circumstances, they were obliged to capitulate and submit to the English. Our Irish Annals record their valiant opposition to the invading hosts, and they were among the last Irish chieftains, who fell under the foreign yoke. Notwithstanding changes of times and fortunes, since the days of their greatness have passed as magnates in the land; still, on the bead-roll of our history in Ireland, many a distinguished man of the name deserves the honour and gratitude of his fellow-countrymen, for public spirit and private worth have never been wanting, when the cause of creed or country needed effort and sacrifice. So may it prove in the future, as it has happened in the past.

Divers may descend to the lowest depths of ocean, and take therefrom only glittering but worthless shells; while the true pearl-fisher, by habit and instinct, will select only those shells filled with valuable pearls. Thus it happens, also, with men of this world, as contra-distinguished from others, who seek pearls of still greater price. Bold, resolute, and vigorous efforts are required to secure the highest prizes of earth or heaven. Dangers

must be incurred in many if not in most cases. Worldling
tempt God's judgments, and at the end, find their hand
empty, a just measure of punishment awaiting thei
transgressions.   The saints obey promptings of duty
and they triumph over all adversities, even when en
countering the greatest trials and dangers; because th
Almighty is ever found on their side, aiding, inspiring
and directing their earthly struggles, with the object o
preparing them for their ultimate end.   They rest witl
God, when called away from this life, and they leav
pious memorials to their clients of the Church militan
in this world.   They pray for us on high, and teach u
by their examples and actions the way that conducts t
everlasting happiness.

THE END.

CPSIA information can be obtained
at www.ICGtesting.com
Printed in the USA
BVHW041132180119
538187BV00016B/1144/P